Keys to Retention

SERVE THE STAFF

THE KEYS TO RETENTION THROUGH HEALTHY SOCIAL EMOTIONAL CULTURE AND CLIMATE

Keys to Retention

SERVE THE STAFF

THE KEYS TO RETENTION THROUGH HEALTHY SOCIAL EMOTIONAL CULTURE AND CLIMATE

ONEDIA NICOLE GAGE, PH. D., CLC

Keys to Retention

Dedication

To the Leadership of schools, please help yourself retain your great staff!

To those who Teach and those who left because this was not in practice yet!

Keep Teaching.

They need you.

You need them.

Thank you!

Keys to Retention

Quotes

"Education is the most powerful weapon which you can use to change the world." - Nelson Mandela

"To teach is to learn twice." - Joseph Joubert

"The beautiful thing about learning is that no one can take it away from you." - B.B. King

"The function of education is to teach one to think intensively and to think critically. Intelligence plus character — that is the goal of true education." - Martin Luther King Jr.

"Education is the most powerful weapon you can use to change the world for the better." - Marian Wright Edelman

LIBRARY OF CONGRESS

SERVE THE STAFF:

The Keys to Retention through Healthy Social Emotional Culture and Climate

All Rights Reserved © 2025

Onedia N. Gage, Ph. D., CLC

No part of this book may be reproduced or transmitted in Any form or by any means, graphic, electronic, or mechanical, Including photocopying, recording, taping, or by any Information storage or retrieval system, without the Permission in writing from the publisher.

Purple Ink, Inc. Press

For Information address:
Purple Ink, Inc.
1202 E. 1st St., 14931,
Humble, TX 77347
www.purpleink.net ♦ onediagage@purpleink.net

Onedia Gage Speaks

www.onediagespeaks.com ♦ onediagage@onediagespeaks.com

ISBN:

978-1-939119-73-5

Printed in the United States

Other Books by
Onedia N. Gage, Ph. D., CLC

Are You Ready for 9th Grade . . . Again? A Family's Guide to Success
As We Grow Together Daily Devotional for Expectant Couples
As We Grow Together Prayer Journal for Expectant Couples
As We Grow Together Bible Study: Her Workbook
As We Grow Together Bible Study: His Workbook
Because I Do: A Working Marriage—Her Workbook
Because I Do: A Working Marriage—His Workbook
The Best 40 Days of My Life: A Journey of Spiritual Renewal
The Blue Print: Poetry for the Soul
From Fat to Fit in 90 Days: A Fitness Journal
From Two to One: The Notebook for the Christian Couple
Hannah's Voice: Powerful Lessons in Prayer
The Heart of a Woman: The Depth of Her Soul
Her Story The Legacy of Her Fight: The Bible Study
Her Story The Legacy of Her Fight: The Devotional
Her Story The Legacy of Her Fight: The Legacy Journal
Her Story The Legacy of Her Fight: Prayers and Journal
I Am.: 90 Days of Powerful Words: Affirmation and Advice for Girls
ily! A Mother-Daughter Relationship Workbook
In 90 Days: What Will You Do?
In Her Own Words: Notebook for the Christian Woman
In Purple Ink: Poetry for the Spirit
In Your Hands: A Dad's Impact on His Daughter's Self-Esteem
Intensive Couples Retreat: Her Workbook
Intensive Couples Retreat: His Workbook
Living A Whole Life: Sermons Which Prompt, Provoke, and Provide Life
Living An Authentic Life
Love Letters to God from a Teenage Girl
The Measure of a Woman: The Details of Her Soul
The Notebook: For Me, About Me, By Me
The Notebook for the Christian Teen
On the Same Team
On This Journey Daily Devotional for Young People
On This Journey Prayer Journal for Young People
On This Journey Prayer Journal for Young People, Vol. 2
One Day More Than We Deserve Prayer Journal for the Growing Christian
Promises, Promises: A Christian Novel

Queen in the Making: 30-Week Bible Study for Teen Girls
Queen in the Making: 30 Week Bible Study for Teen Girls Leader's Guide
The Secrets of My Success: Business Coaching How does she do it? Who does she think she is?
Serve the Staff: The Impact of a Healthy Social-Emotional Climate and Culture
She Spoke Volumes . . . And Then Some
Six Months of Solitude: The Sanctity of Singleness Notebook
Six Months of Solitude: The Sanctity of Singleness Prayers and Journal
There's a Queen Within: Her Journey to Building Self—Worth
Tools for These Times: Timely Sermons for Uncertain Times
The Vision Notebook
Walking Tall with a Broken Life
What Did You Say?: Affirmations. Encouragement. Motivation.
With a Crown and No Home
With An Anointed Voice: The Power of Prayer
A Woman Like Me: A Bible Study for Women to Survive Our Times
A Woman Like Me: A Daily Devotional for Women to Survive Our Times
A Woman Like Me (a sermonic study): Lessons for Us Women
Yielded and Submitted: A Woman's Journey for a Life Dedicated to God
Yielded and Submitted: A Woman's Journey for a Life Dedicated to God An Intimate Study
Yielded and Submitted: A Woman's Journey for a Life Dedicated to God Prayers and Journal

The Nehemiah Character Series

Nehemiah and His Basketball
Nehemiah and His Big Sister
Nehemiah and His Bike
Nehemiah and His Flag Football Team
Nehemiah and His Football
Nehemiah and His Golf Clubs
Nehemiah and Math
Nehemiah and the Bully
Nehemiah and the Busy Day
Nehemiah and the Class Field Trip
Nehemiah and the Substitute for the Substitute

Nehemiah Can Swim
Nehemiah Found the Mud
Nehemiah Reads to Mommy
Nehemiah Writes Just Like Mommy
Nehemiah, the Hot Dog, and the Broccoli
Nehemiah's Family Vacation
Nehemiah's Favorite Teacher Returns to School
Nehemiah's First Day of School
Nehemiah's Sister Moved
Nehemiah's Visit to the Hospital

Keys to Retention

Dear Superintendent and the entire Executive Leadership Team:

There are at least ten priorities that are number one. The only actual priority is to educate the kids. The only way to do that is to retain quality teachers. When the social emotional learning concept was developed, shared and implemented, this caused teachers to give more to students but teachers were already at empty. Now, you want the teacher to consider several additional factors when educating the student.

What about the teacher though? Who nurtures and heals the teacher? Who checks for and consoles the teacher? Who has compassion for the teacher and their needs and life issues? Your teacher is your gold coin. That human asset is your priority. With that being said, what are you able to offer your school-based leadership in order to make this a reality? While you ponder that, let's consider your current state of affairs: your retention is just below 60%. There are schools who have had eight of the 10 positions as substitutes in one year because of turnover for various reasons. This program and practices can only improve the environment which would increase the ability to retain and to attract additional teachers.

Help your schools by infusing the necessary tools and with the necessary money in order to afford the program and the associated activities.

We look forward to your success as a district overall and each school individually.

Sincerely,

Onedia N. Gage, Ph. D., CLC

Former Teacher

Keys to Retention

Dear Principal/Leadership:

You probably leave everyday with many items that you need to do better for tomorrow. This list will always include build relationship with the staff.

At the beginning of one of my school years, my principal took the staff on yellow school buses to the nearest bowling alley. We bowled three games, had some appetizers, and returned to school. As a result, we bonded as a team as well as understood the focus to a comradery and fellowship. This event was unparalleled to any other school year kickoff. I do not need to know the total cost but I can say that he committed to us in a powerful manner. He built a rapport that said be at school, daily and on time, with an amazing work ethic for the benefit of kids, be present on testing days, but if there is an emergency then be grown enough to call me directly on my cell phone. This type of leadership and investment is RARE. He eventually became an area superintendent. He invested in us so that we would invest in his students. And we did!

What does your staff mean to you? What do you want them to do and be for each other? What will they do for your scholars if you invest in them in ways that they have never seen?

Well, let's see what happens.

Do what these pages say.

Fully.

Completely.

Without holding anything back.

Watch the results.

Keys to Retention

Let me know how I can help. I am available to come and train your staff on how to execute what is in these pages. Please let me know how I can help you to be successful.

Sincerely,

Onedia N. Gage, Ph. D., CLC

Former Teacher

Keys to Retention

Table of Contents

Letter to District Personnel	15
Letter to Principal	17
The Why: Why do you need this	25
What Will You and Your Staff Achieve with This New Culture and Climate	29
A Data Driven Decision	31
Leaders Lead from the Front	37
The School that Caused the Need for a Plan to Change the Social Emotional, Culture and Climate of a School	43
The Ideal School	47
A Call to Action	49
Sample Plan	51
Proposed Budget	59
Serve the Staff	63
Planning Pages	65
Resources	91
Acknowledgements	93
About the Servant	95
Book the Servant	97

KEYS TO RETENTION

SERVE.
THE.
STAFF.

Keys to Retention

The Why: Why Do You Need This

Social emotional culture and climate wellness is defined as a climate and culture where family, fun, and wellness is happening at your location. The definition includes how to help relieve the stress of the job, inclusive of making the actual environment less stressful even if the work has not changed.

Retention is important for the health of your organization. Burnout is real. Creating a sense of belonging is important. Making people feel valued is critical for the loyalty that you want to build when you have a team that is good but needs to be great.

The SEL investment should offer back the desire for the environment in which they work and serve your students.

In the following proposal, you will see the benefits. People want to like where they spend 35% to 50% of their lives. A great place to work will increase attendance, timeliness, and work ethic. Unhappy employees steal from your organization and will forego loyalty in order to change what your school can achieve.

Imagine a school where the actual majority of your teachers and staff arrive to work on time, complete their assigned tasks, invest in the students at a high level, and voluntarily volunteers for additional duties that is not attached to extra pay.

Imagine being able to actually delegate to people who are willing to do the work with diligence and fidelity, with the most important being to teach the students. When you imagine the school with outstanding results in all categories, for both students and staff, this school has authentic positive climate and culture, without regards of the leadership.

When the culture is of excellence then when leadership does transition, the team will continue the social emotional practices that are a part of the culture. When a new leader arrives, then they can only add to the current activities because the culture is strong and stable.

Just a note about the strength of culture: when a leader leaves, the measure of its culture will be based on whether that culture will sustain into the next leadership regime. I witnessed a school that changed leadership during the summer. Upon arrival of the new principal, all of the previous procedures stopped but was not replaced with anything new. The culture has failed and became absent.

The idea is to ensure that the culture offers the platform for developing a strong culture and climate and then sustaining that culture. They will also consider the climate and will take steps in order to adjust the climate in order to make the organization comfortable and attractive.

This work will drive away the toxicity that has established itself on your property. This toxicity is what stalls or stops your student achievement through staff apathy. This toxicity shows up through people who are negative in the overall atmosphere and those who stall progress of the building's goals. This toxicity needs to be eliminated so that the building can reach its goals in a manner which does not include any negativity.

The Why is that these activities and this investment will change the mind and heart of everyone in the building. This will spread like wildfire. Your building will BE the place to work; the place to NEVER leave. It will also be the place to protect, serve, and celebrate for all that is has become. And will continue to be.

You need this:

    Serve the Staff!

Keys to Retention

What Will You and Your Staff Achieve with This New Culture and Climate

Imagine that school A is an F rated campus. This school has the lowest scores of its districts twenty schools. The school has an issue retaining its staff with a thirty (30) teacher turnover each school year, often opening the school year with vacancies in core subjects. The staff satisfaction survey is the lowest of the entire district.

The students aren't learning. The teachers aren't teaching. The teachers are having attendance issues: late arrival and excessive absences. Thes student's behavior is terrible. Suspensions are high. Morale is low. The staff does not have any school spirit. The staff rarely participates in school sponsored events, including the sports events for the students.

Imagine that there are some changes that are made that will change the culture and climate of the organization. This change will change all of that negativity and low levels of morale and motivation. The change will also cause negative people to part from the organization.

We already have a teacher shortage so what will you do when you are not able to staff your school?

Keys to Retention

This new effort will help you with retention of your current staff because your staff will have better morale. Imagine your team wanting to recruit teachers to your school for you.

When you consider the factors which shape the school's reputation, the one that is the most powerful is how the teacher's feel about where they work. When the teachers like where they work, they will recruit their friends, family, and previous colleagues and classmates to work there. Teachers can cause people to come or to completely avoid your school and your district.

A Data Driven Decision

When this plan was initially offered to a principal, his response was, "It is nice but I don't have any money to do this." When he was offered fundraising ideas, he refused.

As a principal/decision maker, there are so many more factors to consider other than money. Building a better culture requires the data driven decisions that we force our staff and teams to consider.

Here is a short list of data points:

- Do you have teacher vacancies in core subjects?
- Do you have more than 10% staff attrition each year?
- Do you have excessive absenteeism around Fridays, Mondays and holidays?
- Do you have excessive tardiness?
- Are you at least 10% of teachers at your after-school events?
- Do you have the same teachers hosting tutorials?
- Do you struggle to offer after school tutorials because the teachers don't stay to offer them?
- Is your campus academically failing?
- Are there more than five grievances on the campus each year?

This is a short list of low morale indicators.

These are the data points that indicate that you do not have their full attention or investment of your current team. Consider the person(s) who influences your campus. The entire campus moves because that person(s) endorses the event(s). This is the person who will also influence your team. If they are not someone that you trust, then they need to go. Or they need to be influenced to assist with the changes. Some leaders do not want to consider the influencer, whether negative or positive but they have a huge impact on your campus. Which also means that your initiatives could fail without their nod of approval. This makes change hard but not impossible so you need to make this change so that your campus is free to perform at the highest possible levels.

There was one campus which was run by four women. They worked on three different hallways, in two different content areas. They were the influencers in the school. If you did not contact them, then your events were not well attended, if at all. They collaborated with each other and a few others, but they were in charge. This is hard for some to embrace but you may want to inventory your staff for influencers if no one is on your mind at this time.

Overcoming that negative person will be a huge boost for the campus morale. This person is preventing your campus from being a high performing campus. Your influencer will also help with this person(s). If your campus is below a B, all parties need to be listening to you. Otherwise, they are all maintaining that below average performance. A healthy influencer would be helping the campus to move forward as a better campus performance, which includes getting people on board for the campus positive needs. If not, then they are the problem.

If you cannot afford this plan and its accompanying activities, then you cannot afford not to do it. If you don't have the financial budget, then you are not going to be in a good place as a campus either. Your team does not understand budgets, maybe you don't either. Either way, there needs to be a change. Happy staff members will use their outside sources to fund your campus. They all have a network. If they don't use their network to help you, then they don't believe in your campus or in you. As you consider your goals and direction for your school and scholars, what is your ultimate goal? If your goals have fallen short for consecutive quarters or semesters or years, then you should reconsider your direction and your approach. This will be helpful to the overall direction of the achievement that you are attempting to achieve.

The data should determine the implementation of the plan because nothing else has worked. You don't have anything to lose if you take this safe chance to increase your opportunities for success.

The data needs a significant shift. There's a national teacher shortage and there will be one for at least a decade, until 2035. Some principals are using virtual teachers and substitutes to offer tier one instruction, of which the principal and team does not have any control over the curriculum. This is frightening. However, your perception does not matter because if this virtual option did not exist, who would be teaching these kids? If the answer is nobody, then we may want to consider this effort as something to retain those Very Important Teachers, your VIT.

Teachers are in a competitive environment. You don't control any incentives that the district may or may not offer. You don't control their salary. You don't control the district calendar. You do control the climate and culture of your building. You need to infuse some greatness within the building. Again, there should be a retention bonus for principals, but again that is not in your control.

Keys to Retention

Retention is a report card grade. Furthermore, when your school has had more applicants than positions, that is a good report card. Otherwise, you are in competition with hundreds of other schools which have many amenities. Each math teacher has 4–6 offers–they can make their own mark wherever they are. They will be employed so this makes your school attractive.

Remember that three questions will be asked at each interview: 1) What is your academic status or grade at this time? 2) What are you doing to improve this grade? 3) What are you doing for the wellness and well-being of your teachers?

You need to have a concrete plan for each of those questions. Remember that your competition is also reading this book. Some are willing to do what you are not. Some principals are doing what you won't. There's been a transition and some principals, and even districts, have missed it. Teachers are now to be handled like first round draft picks.

When division one colleges and universities are recruiting to persuade the top players in the country to accept their offers of a full tuition, room, and housing scholarship in exchange to put their health in danger in order to play football. Fifty-three student athletes "volunteer" in exchange for the "great" education each year for multiple years at almost all of the colleges and universities in the world, especially America. One last reminder, these top ranked players from all over the nation are seniors in high school. These athletes are being flown across the country, picked up in limousines, and fed some of the finest food that the area offers, along with tours, special conversations, and alumni of the program in order to close the deal. These are teenagers with the red carpet rolled out for them.

What are we doing for our "first round draft spots?" Not that. Do they know that they are wanted? Needed? Appreciated? What can be done in order to make it work?

People make decisions based on non-tangible details, so how they feel about the work location and how they are treated will be the leading decision-making detail in the decision-making process. Some people aren't happy with their relationships but they won't leave. They have a biological family that they cannot leave. But for this job, they can and will leave. The data highlights that is a fact. The exit rate for educators is one of the highest in the country in 2021, 2022, and 2023. This is a problem because we are not certifying teachers at the same rate of those who are leaving the field.

You are in competition with everything so you may want to consider that if we are not presenting some better environments then we will lose more teachers than we will be able to find to replacements for. Let's figure out how to make that happen.

There are costs regarding recruiting, hiring, and onboarding. There are costs associated with this plan, which will consider as retention and recruitment efforts. From a budget perspective, your campus may not have all of the funds needed for this to work so you need to petition the district and your community for some help.

Keys to Retention

You are attempting to save the district thousands of dollars. When you address the community, you need to remind them that these teachers contribute to their profit margins, and that they are educating the next team members and customers.

This plan is designed, if done properly, to benefit the community who will appreciate our investment in their community as well as what they will receive as a result of that investment. We need to raise funds in order to make this happen. We need to ask for help in order to make this a reality.

Social emotional wellness and building a better culture and climate is far less expensive than the recruitment and replacement cost for new teachers.

LEADERS LEAD FROM THE FRONT

As a leadership team, we need to lead by doing what we ask of others. We teach many strategies, some of which are excellent for building relationships and increasing performance. There are behaviors that we suggest/require from our teachers that we should also do with our teams and staff members.

What if we practiced what they are expected to do?

Standing at the threshold, getting to know each staff member, agreeing on what to teach each of them, and finding a connection with each of them.

Where can you personally greet your staff daily so that you see their face and body language? How can you do this?

As a classroom teacher, I greet each of my students at the door because I needed to see exactly the mood that they were in so that I would know what I would expect from them today. When I see someone that does appear to be a 100%, I have that person step to the side so that we can talk before we start the lesson.

As a principal, you may choose to visit their classrooms or send for them at their conference. Or have the Instructional Specialist or substitute cover their class to offer them a break from their situation.

If I was not able to make progress with that student, I employed some help, like the counselor or favorite teacher. Similarly, we as leaders need to consider that we need to reach our staff in the same way. Our staff needs to be equally invested in, as we invest in our students. Will you tell your team members that they care about their needs and their concerns, then you are truly investing in the whole person. This is the difference between being involved and being committed.

There is an adage about the chicken and the pig regarding breakfast. The chicken was involved. The pig was committed. Regarding your staff, what will your staff feel if you were committed to them in that manner? What will your staff feel if you do this? How does this change how your building performs? How do they respond differently now that they know how much you care? Ae you ready to change your building? This is a great start.

What happens when you remember what they share with you? What does it mean to them when you remember their kids' names? What happens when you ask about the progress of a life changing event? How does it make you feel when it happens to you? You probably feel invested in and valued. You are comfortable with your progress and your supervisor has expressed confidence in you. You feel valued and are compelled to do a good job.

Whether the thought process is practical or not, there are people who feel that if you do not value them then they do not have to do a good job. While this is faulty logic, many use this logic in their workplace. They seem to be void of the obligation to do the job that they were hired for and for which they are paid without interruption. Their work performance, including arrival and departure times, is attached to how they feel about you and your environment. Again, consider your Friday and Monday attendance rates. Please consider that because you know the thought process, you can work to change the narrative.

As the leader, lead from the front. Greet your staff every morning; either at their rooms or at the time clock or sign in station; unless there is one door that they all enter.

Know something about each of them so that you can talk about it to remain connected. They will value that connection and you will reap the benefits. What will you personally and intentionally teach each of your staff members? Conversely, what do you need to learn from them?

Do you know the professional goal of each of your team members? If not, when will you know? What are you doing in order to help them attain their goals? Are you coaching them so that they will be ready for the role they desire? If not, then you are failing that person. Most people do not perform well if they do not have a goal. As their immediate supervisor, you should know that goal and be able to help them to reach that goal(s). Again, is your investment ethic at its optimal level in order to get the most from your staff?

What talents are on your campus? What do they do in their free time? What are those gifts and talents are they willing to share with you? To further the mission, vision, and values of this organization/team? Do they feel like they are a member, a real member of this team?

Keys to Retention

Do you remember the first time that you were surprised and hurt by the resignation of a staff person? You did not know because you are not in touch with your teams. There are some of the most insignificant events or missteps which cause people to seek alternative employment.

You have also realized by now that you will not know everything and most people don't tell the truth, at least not the whole truth.

As a result of leading from the front, your staff will start to increase productivity and investment because they notice this change. They will respond differently. Those that still don't see the overall vision and contribute accordingly may be on the wrong ship. It may then be time to change team members.

As a leader, I have mostly promoted from my team and trained everyone with what they need to be successful anywhere. I had a team member named James. James wanted to transfer to another store. I offered my recommendation to the receiving store. He was hired. He came home from college on break and dropped by. We converse. I was not ready for what happened next though. He said thank you. I was mildly surprised but nothing overwhelming. He's then apologized. He shared the conversation that he had with the management team. I'm excited based on what I hear then he shocks the world: 'I took your leadership for granted and certainly underestimated your worth and power.' All that I could muster was 'wow.' He goes on to add that he admired my courage. The receiving store was overwhelmed with how much he knew how to do. He asked them, 'Didn't everyone get trained on everything?' They responded no. They elaborated that what I had done was unprecedented and forward-thinking, and definitely unexpected.

Serve the Staff

James said he had no idea that I did what no one else had, that I had not withheld anything from my team, and that I had invested in them in that manner.

I responded with my philosophy: I cross train everyone, mostly because my teams are small. I need everyone's help. This is more equitable for the team as well as when you are working. There's a choice of duties which helps the work go faster. More importantly, because of that and one other experience, my teams are highly sought after.

Likewise, your reputation is based on how many people you promote, and how they perform when they transfer. You might want to consider the reputation that you have based on how you coach and train your team members. Tell them what they don't know, tell them what they need to know, and tell them how to navigate the nuances of our profession. Help them grow. When you help others grow, you will have achieved the goal. They may also stay.

The School that Caused the Need for a Plan to Change the Social Emotional and Culture and Climate of a School

Let me tell you about a school. This may sound familiar or maybe you have never heard of it, but there is a school that exists that is the foundation of this movement.

Also, just because it is not your school today, make sure that you infuse and implement some, or all, of these elements so that this school is never yours.

The school is underperforming - it's last in the district. In all categories. The absences are high on Fridays, Mondays and before and after all holidays. The student absences are also high. The investment in the school is low.

The school is on the watch list by the district and the State education agency. There are issues with instruction and student compliance. The systems which make a regular school function do not exist. State Testing does not start on time. The testing protocols are sloppy. Teachers call out on testing days. Secure testing areas that are supposed to be restricted are violated without penalty. The testing irregularities are regular.

Keys to Retention

Teachers have become apathetic. They do not care enough to do anything extra. They do not want to hold tutorials for students even if the school is paying for the extra time. The teachers are distrustful of the administrative team because they do not take action in matters of discipline for unruly students.

Teachers lack zeal and zest, compassion and forgiveness for the students you need an extension of grace for.

The teachers are on edge, considering the retirement option, as well as a career change. They have closely examined their commitment to education and have decided to rescind their allegiance. This low morale will be evident when the leadership asks more from them. The teachers will say no, become defiant, and file grievances. They start to quote the law. They do not do anything extra. They stop covering the inadequacies of the school.

They don't attend extracurricular activities unless they are personally invited by a student that matters to them. They would quit mid-year if they were not a consequence of State sanctions on their teacher certificates. They may quit sometimes without regards for the possibilities of sanction. The school is not clean. The pride is so poor that teachers will walk over trash. They do not provide any solutions to the issues that exist. They do not have any faith in the leadership or the students.

The school does not have any positive press or any good news. They are not on any achievers such as National Merit Sholars. The school is at the bottom of all lists. Achievement is absent. Absenteeism is high. People do not have a good opinion of the school. People with average or better students move to better neighborhoods with better schools so that their students don't have to go to this school. They open the school year every year with a dozen vacancies and often have to split classes due to substitutes not appearing at the school.

Your goal is to find out what your school's reputation and what the statistics are. Once you know then set the goals in order to change those numbers. These numbers only change when some DRASTIC changes are made.

Keys to Retention

The Ideal School

dream if you will . . . a great school

Teachers with exponential talent that they willingly share. When they offer to share their talents and gifts, you are receptive and accept those gifts. They have great results of top test scores, 95% attendance rate, and great parent involvement. The school is clean. The parking lot is clean. The paint is fresh. The students come to school on time. They do not roam the halls. They attend tutorials when they need extra help with a content area. Teachers voluntarily stay for tutorials. They stay after school hours so they can call parents and provide feedback to them about their students.

The teachers are not exhausted, overwhelmed, or complaining. They are excited, involved, and innovative. Lesson plans are submitted on time to the portal. All classrooms are covered with print rich materials that extend the learning. Some students are excited about learning and they are excelling at the difficult subjects, especially math.

Even you are excited to come to work. You don't avoid certain professionals. You have positive and timely responses. You actually are able to mentor and coach, providing timely feedback. You're able to complete meetings and have complete conversations because emergencies are irregular.

The school celebrates every birthday and mourns every death; celebrates every birth and honors every retirement.

Keys to Retention

You rarely take work home. You don't avoid anyone's emails.

You won't ever control the cafeteria menu but there are not any discipline issues at lunch. The students do make social media videos. All assigned personnel attend lunch duty and they forge relationships with the students. You have started to allow lunch time activities and celebrations versus the silent lunch you previously enforced.

Your school wins awards. You enter contests and they are proud to represent the school and even prouder when they win. They are proud of their contribution to the school's history and to help upgrade the school's reputation and legacy.

Your building is in good physical and fiscal condition. Your repairs are completed a timely fashion. Your school is used for district professional development. People do not laugh when your school's name is mentioned. Alumni volunteer to help your school with what students' need and fundraising.

Lastly, you have plenty of money to do EVERYTHING that you need and want to do. Ultimately, you are no longer at the bottom of the list - on any list.

# A Call to Action

Decide.

The first thing to do is to decide to take action. When I introduced this to my former principal, he said no. His excuses were: 'who has the time? who are you going to work with? There needs to be an assistant principal involved as the leader. I don't have any money for this.' Excuses. This is not an option when your school is not successful.

Assign a Champion.

You need a champion, maybe even form a committee, but this work needs a captain, a real leader. This person needs to be the POSITIVE influencer of this work. The school will move and begin to transform. They need to have unequivocal support. They will need excellent productivity so that others will want to follow. A teacher of the year runner-up will be a good idea for this position.

Establish a Budget.

This will require money. You also need to allow the champion and the team to write grants, letters of solicitation to the neighboring businesses, and any necessary fundraisers in order to fund and properly support this effort. Please be sure to supply them with the rules and the training needed in order to collect funds and how to properly set up an account for those expenditures.

Watch and Support the Work.

Be prepared for the naysayers to approach you. Be prepared to protect your team. Be ready to share the pictures and the work of your team and to be honest about the results.

Wait for the Results.

Be prepared for the viewpoint of and appreciation of the staff. Don't be afraid to ask for the results that you desire. If the behavior has not changed for the individual teacher/staff member, then be prepared to hold that individual(s) accountable, which may require a simple conversation or an entire separation plan. The right people need to be on the team so that exceptional results can be realized.

Praise and Adoration.

Thank your team and the leader. Use some of those same funds to offer the leader a token of your appreciation. Survey your staff about the progress.

Sample Plan

1. Celebrate birthdays each month. Usually on the first Friday of each month. At all lunches.

    a. Cake

    b. Mocktails in the SEL room or the teacher's lounge.

2. Perfect Attendance

    a. Monthly

       i. All recognized with a certificate

       ii. The month's entries will be entered into a drawing for

          1. lunch with an assistant principal

          2. extra conference period

    b. End of Semester

       i. Persons with the most entries will be drawn for 5 persons to have lunch with the CAP/DOI (Curriculum Assistant Principal)

    c. End of Year

       i. Draw 5 names for lunch with Principal.

       ii. All other names in the drawing will receive a bonus conference period for this year to be covered by substitute, AP, specialist

       iii. Top person with most months: NO DUTY STATION FOR NEXT YEAR.

3. Fitness Challenge

    a. Monthly $10/person

        i. Highest percentage of weight loss wins 75% of the money (the other 25% of the money will go into the sunshine fund for staff needs)

        ii. Weigh in on Mondays

        iii. Winner announced on the last day of month

        iv. Starts at the first of each month

4. Line dancing class

    a. Tuesday and Thursday of each week

    b. FREE

    c. Cafeteria

    d. 3—4 PM

5. Teacher Appreciation Fridays

    a. A token every Friday (this will vary)

    b. Popcorn will be twice a month

6. Breakfast for the department of the month

7. Lunch as a campus

    a. August

    b. October

    c. November

    d. December

    e. January

f. February

g. April

h. May

8. Door decorating

We will decorate for the assigned theme. Decorations stay up about 2 weeks. We can have a competition to be awarded at the end of the year. We cannot decorate each holiday due to the paper allocation and time. Moving the decorations around by hall should have a pride effect for the hallway/content area.

    a. September: Scholarship—English

    b. October: Academically themed—Science

    c. November: Grateful—Social Studies

    d. December: Winter Wonderland—SPED

    e. February: Love—Math

    f. March: Special Spring—CTE

    g. April: The test is coming—Fine Arts, JROTC, Athletics

    h. WHOLE SCHOOL

        i. Homecoming

        ii. Favorite senior athlete (before football senior night)

9. Pep Rallies

    a. First game

    b. Homecoming

c. Senior night

d. Last game/playoff celebration

e. Each playoff game

    i. The further we go, we will need to add a student bus and decorate the team bus(ses)

f. Spring sports (2)

10. Team Building

    a. Family Movie Night Auditorium

        i. Once each semester

        ii. Open snack bar

            1. Mocktails

            2. Popcorn

            3. Candy

        iii. Saturday, 5PM

    b. Bowling

        i. Once each semester

        ii. Teams by choice

    c. Off Campus Events (These may be self-pay. At the time of reservations, discounts should be discussed.)

        i. Ziplining in Austin

        ii. Fiesta Texas in SA

        iii. Galveston Beach

        iv. Boat Ride

        v. Beer Garden

vi. Wine Tasting and Tour

11. Small Gestures that Mean the Most

    a. Personal notes

    b. Serving them food at a buffet

    c. Covering their class

    d. Co-teaching

12. Teacher Holiday Gift Baskets

13. Teacher Appreciation Week Extravaganza

Keys to Retention

Keys to Retention

The Proposed Budget

I mentioned that the original principal stated that he did not have the money to make this happen. What he did not do was ask what could be done. What he should have been asking is how do you propose that we do this. When the person who brings this to you is prepared to do the work: LET THEM DO IT!!!!

I know that the principal has the big glasses on, however if you do not consider weaving this into your year's plan, you will wonder what would have happened.

Let's examine the school's budget for what can be allocated to this event. Next, let's write proposals for surrounding businesses for donations. Next, we will seek grants for this need of social emotional wellness and retention for teachers. Then, we will fundraise through various district approved means in order to get this done. As a hail mary, we will solicit the excess inventory of national companies for our Teacher Holiday Gift Baskets and Teacher Appreciation Extravaganza. Finally, we will seek other community partners and parents in order to fund the fuel for a great team.

Use the following pages in order to start the planning process for what you will give teachers.

Keys to Retention

Keys to Retention

SERVE THE STAFF

As a staff member, I remember not liking the environment and being envious of other schools and their gifts for teacher appreciation. These events and other forms of appreciation are sacred and that information becomes a reason why teachers stay in the building for years unless they are promoted or they leave the profession.

Consider what the corporate environment and private industry provide their employees. Corporations budget for gifts, marketing materials, as well as celebrations. Corporations give/issue polo shirts and t-shirts to their employees so that they can wear them. It is marketing and company retention. They gift their employees with gifts at the holidays such as turkeys, gift cards, and other items which demonstrates appreciation. In the summer, they host company events. They offer company bonuses based on performance and as a part of profit sharing. They form intramural sports groups they compete with other companies.

The company with the best gifts and bonuses is the one with the fewest unfilled positions and with the healthiest hiring practices. Yes, this will cost you, but you are already paying some of the costs that you cannot afford. Whatever is required to improve the morale is worth the investment and the effort.

Companies will spend money in order to increase profitability and maintain comradery and cohesiveness. Teams are healthier when they have events and gifts to work for and look forward to.

Keys to Retention

Events are really impactful. Family events also stimulate camaraderie. I received some bad advice once about treat your team like family. That's terrible advice but the statement warranted editing: treat them like friends and people that you love. The family piece was the bad part of the advice - most people don't have a healthy family experience so the work environment does not need to mimic anything negative.

You don't want your team to think of all of the negative here as compared to the positive elsewhere.

Work hard on this. Focus on this and the positive that will come.

Serve the Staff.

THE PLANNING PAGES

What are your thoughts? What are your desires and decisions? What are you concerned about? Use the following pages in order to start the ball rolling. May the best be with you.

_____

_____

_____

_____

_____

_____

_____

_____

_____

_____

_____

_____

_____

_____

_____

_____

_____

_____

_____

Keys to Retention

SERVE THE STAFF

Keys to Retention

Serve the Staff

Keys to Retention

Serve the Staff

Keys to Retention

Keys to Retention

Keys to Retention

KEYS TO RETENTION

SERVE THE STAFF

Keys to Retention

Keys to Retention

Keys to Retention

Keys to Retention

Keys to Retention

Keys to Retention

Resources

If You Don't Feed the Teachers, They Eat the Students! Guide to Success for Administrators and Teachers

Neila A. Connors

Essential Truths for Principals

Danny Steele and Todd Whitaker

What Great Principals Do Differently

Todd Whitaker

Keys to Retention

Acknowledgements

God, thank You for Your plans for me. Thank You for **Serve the Staff**, and choosing me to complete Your project. I just want to please You, God. Thank You for continuing to anoint me and to invest in me and my gifts, which keep surprising me. Thank You for loving and forgiving me.

Jordan and Nehemiah, thank you for supporting me and my endeavors. Thank you for loving me, especially when I do nothing without a pen and a clipboard, thank you for enduring my late nights, your ideas, the sounding board, the love and the support. Thank you for celebrating our legacy.

To my prayer partners and to my accountability partners, thank you for the long talks and the powerful prayers and the encouragement.

To the readers who this will reach and empower and touch and affect, may these words empower you and help you reach some resolve. May you be inspired to achieve your goals and dreams. May you enhance your relationship with God so that your other relationships will also improve. May you enhance your self-esteem through prayer and study. May you have courage and peace. Share love the best you can until you can share love without reservation.

Keys to Retention

About the Servant

You were a teacher. Remember what you said that you wished your principal would do, now do that. We are here for you.

Do not hesitate to ask, to engage at a high level of participation, anticipating the best for you!

@onediangage (twitter) ♦ onediagage@onediagage.com ♦ facebook.com/onediagage

youtube.com/onediagage ♦ blogtalkradio.com/onediagage ♦ ongage (instagram)

www.coachonedia.com ♦ www.onediagagespeaks.com

Keys to Retention

SERVE THE STAFF

ADVOCATE ♦ TEACHER ♦ FACILITATOR
CONFERENCE SPEAKER ♦ PANELIST ♦ WORKSHOP LEADER

To invite Coach Gage to speak at your Convocation, Professional Development,

Or other events,

Please contact us at: www.onediagagespeaks.com

@onediangage (twitter) ♦ onediagage@onediagagespeaks.com ♦ facebook.com/onediagage

youtube.com/onediagage ♦ ongage (Instagram)

Gage, Ph. D., CLC | **97**

Keys to Retention

Publishing

Do you have a book you want to write, but do not know what to do?

Do you have a book you need to publish but do not know how to start?

Would publishing move your career forward?

Let us help

onediagage@purpleink.net ♦ www.purpleink.net

713.705.5530 ♦ 281.740.5143

www.ingramcontent.com/pod-product-compliance
Lightning Source LLC
Chambersburg PA
CBHW061803070526
44586CB00023B/2695